Soups & Stews

Dublin Coddle

½ pound fresh Brussels sprouts
2 pounds potatoes, peeled and sliced ½ inch thick
1 pound Irish pork sausage,* sliced into 1-inch pieces
1 pound smoked ham, cut into cubes
3 medium onions, cut into 1-inch pieces
½ pound fresh baby carrots
1 teaspoon dried thyme
½ teaspoon black pepper

*Irish pork sausage is similar to fresh garlic-flavored bratwurst. If unavailable, substitute
1 pound regular pork sausage and add 1 clove minced garlic with other ingredients in step 2.

1. Cut stem from each Brussels sprout and pull off outer bruised
leaves. Cut an "X" deep into stem end of each sprout with paring
knife.

2. Place potatoes, sausage, ham, sprouts, onions, carrots, thyme and
pepper in large Dutch oven. Add enough water to just barely cover
ingredients. Bring to a boil over high heat. Reduce heat to medium.
Cover and simmer 20 minutes. Uncover; continue cooking 15 minutes
or until vegetables are tender. Remove from heat.

3. Cool slightly. Skim any fat from surface of liquid by lightly pulling
clean paper towel across surface, letting paper towel absorb fat. To
serve, spoon meat and vegetables into individual bowls along with
some broth.   *Makes 8 to 10 servings*

Dublin Coddle

Beef Stew with Bacon, Onion and Sweet Potatoes

- 1 pound beef stew meat (1-inch chunks)
- 1 can (about 14 ounces) beef broth
- 2 medium sweet potatoes, peeled, cut into 2-inch chunks*
- 1 large onion, cut into 1½-inch chunks
- 2 slices thick-cut bacon, diced
- 1 teaspoon dried thyme
- 1 teaspoon salt
- ¼ teaspoon black pepper
- 2 tablespoons cornstarch
- 2 tablespoons water

*You may substitute 12 to 13 ounces of carrots or white potatoes, cut into 2-inch chunks.

Slow Cooker Directions

1. Coat slow cooker with nonstick cooking spray. Combine all ingredients except cornstarch and water in slow cooker; mix well.

2. Cover; cook on LOW 7 to 8 hours or on HIGH 4 to 5 hours or until meat and vegetables are tender.

3. With slotted spoon, transfer beef and vegetables to serving bowl; cover with foil to keep warm.

4. Turn slow cooker to HIGH. Combine cornstarch and water until smooth. Stir into juices; cover and cook 15 minutes or until thickened. Spoon sauce over beef and vegetables.   *Makes 4 servings*

Beef Stew with Bacon, Onion
and Sweet Potatoes

Chunky Chicken Stew

1 teaspoon olive oil
1 small onion, diced
1 cup thinly sliced carrots
1 cup chicken broth
1 can (about 14 ounces) diced tomatoes
1 cup diced cooked chicken breast
3 cups sliced kale or baby spinach leaves

1. Heat oil in large saucepan over medium-high heat. Add onion; cook and stir about 5 minutes or until golden brown. Stir in carrots and broth; bring to a boil.

2. Reduce heat to low; simmer, uncovered, 5 minutes. Add tomatoes with juice; simmer 5 minutes or until carrots are tender. Add chicken; heat through. Add kale, stirring until wilted. Simmer 1 minute. Ladle into bowls. *Makes 2 servings*

Creamy Curry Carrot Soup

2 tablespoons butter
2 to 3 teaspoons curry powder
1 teaspoon salt
1 medium onion, finely chopped
4 medium carrots, shredded
3 (14½-ounce) cans chicken broth, divided
3 cups cooked long grain rice
1 cup whipping cream

Melt butter in large stockpot over medium-high heat. Blend in curry powder and salt, stirring constantly for 30 seconds. Add onion and carrots; sauté 7 to 9 minutes, stirring frequently.

Carefully spoon mixture into blender or food processor. Add 1 can broth to vegetables; blend but don't purée.

Return mixture to stockpot; add remaining 2 cans broth and rice. Heat over medium-high heat until hot, about 5 minutes. Remove from heat and stir in cream. *Makes 8 servings*

*Favorite recipe from **USA Rice***

Hearty Sausage Stew

¼ cup olive oil
4 carrots, chopped
1 onion, cut into quarters
1 cup chopped celery
2 cloves garlic, finely chopped
1 teaspoon finely chopped fennel
  Salt and black pepper to taste
12 small new potatoes
1 pound mushrooms, cut into halves
2 cans (12 ounces each) diced tomatoes, undrained
1 can (8 ounces) tomato sauce
1 tablespoon dried oregano leaves
1 pound **HILLSHIRE FARM® Polska Kielbasa,*** sliced

*Or use any variety Hillshire Farm® Smoked Sausage.

Heat oil in heavy skillet over medium-high heat; add carrots, onion, celery, garlic, fennel, salt and pepper. Sauté until vegetables are soft. Add potatoes, mushrooms, tomatoes with liquid, tomato sauce and oregano; cook 20 minutes over low heat. Add Polska Kielbasa; simmer 15 minutes or until heated through.   *Makes 6 servings*

Farm Fresh Tip: Did you know? If you don't have 2 cups of tomato sauce, you can substitute ¾ cup of tomato paste mixed into 1 cup of water.

Creamy Slow Cooker
Seafood Chowder

1 quart (4 cups) half-and-half
2 cans (14½ ounces each) whole white potatoes, drained and cubed
2 cans (10¾ ounces) condensed cream of mushroom soup,
    undiluted
1 bag (16 ounces) frozen hash brown potatoes, thawed
1 medium onion, minced
½ cup (1 stick) butter, diced
1 teaspoon salt
1 teaspoon black pepper
5 cans (about 8 ounces each) whole oysters, drained and rinsed
2 cans (about 6 ounces each) minced clams
2 cans (about 4 ounces each) cocktail shrimp, drained and rinsed

Slow Cooker Directions

1. Combine half-and-half, canned potatoes, soup, hash browns, onion, butter, salt and pepper in 6-quart slow cooker. Mix well.

2. Add oysters, clams and shrimp; stir gently.

3. Cover; cook on LOW 4 to 5 hours. *Makes 8 to 10 servings*

Creamy Slow Cooker
Seafood Chowder

Hearty Lentil and Root Vegetable Stew

1 cup dried red lentils, rinsed and sorted

8 ounces turnip root, scrubbed and cut into 1-inch cubes (about 1½ cups)

1 medium yellow onion, cut into ½-inch wedges

2 medium carrots, cut into 1-inch pieces

1 medium red bell pepper, cut into 1-inch pieces

½ teaspoon dried oregano

⅛ teaspoon red pepper flakes

2 cans (about 14 ounces each) chicken broth

1 tablespoon olive oil

½ teaspoon salt

4 slices bacon, crisp-cooked and crumbled

½ cup finely chopped green onions

Slow Cooker Directions

1. Combine lentils, turnip, onion, carrots, bell pepper, oregano, red pepper flakes in 3½- to 4-quart slow cooker. Pour broth over top.

2. Cover; cook on LOW 6 hours or on HIGH 3 hours or until lentils are tender.

3. Stir in olive oil and salt. Sprinkle bacon and green onions over top of each serving.   *Makes 8 servings*

Hearty Lentil and Root
Vegetable Stew

Beer and Cheese Soup

2 to 3 slices pumpernickel or rye bread
3 tablespoons cornstarch
3 tablespoons water
¼ cup finely chopped onion
1 tablespoon butter or margarine
¾ teaspoon dried thyme
2 cloves garlic, minced
1 can (about 14 ounces each) chicken broth
1 cup beer
6 ounces American cheese, shredded or diced
4 to 6 ounces sharp Cheddar cheese, shredded
½ teaspoon paprika
1 cup milk

1. Preheat oven to 425°F. Slice bread into ½-inch cubes; place on baking sheet. Bake 10 to 12 minutes, or until crisp, stirring once; set aside.

2. While bread is in oven, combine cornstarch and water in small bowl; set aside. Cook and stir onion, butter, thyme and garlic in 3-quart saucepan over medium-high heat 3 to 4 minutes or until onion is tender.

3. Add broth; bring to a boil. Stir in beer, cheeses and paprika. Reduce heat to low; whisk in milk and cornstarch mixture. Stir until cheese melts and soup bubbles and thickens. Ladle into bowls. Top with croutons.   *Makes 6 servings*

Prep and Cook Time: 20 minutes

Sweet Potato Stew

1 cup chopped yellow onion
1 cup chopped celery
1 cup grated peeled sweet potato
1 cup vegetable broth or water
2 slices bacon, crisp-cooked and crumbled
1 cup half-and-half
    Salt and black pepper
¼ cup minced fresh parsley

Slow Cooker Directions

1. Place onion, celery, sweet potato, broth and bacon in 3-quart slow cooker. Cover; cook on LOW 6 hours.

2. Increase heat to HIGH. Add half-and-half, using just enough to bring stew to desired consistency. Add more water, if needed. Cook 30 minutes on HIGH or until hot.

3. Season to taste with salt and pepper. Stir in parsley.

Makes 4 servings

Ham and Cauliflower Chowder

1 bag (16 ounces) BIRDS EYE® frozen Cauliflower
2 cans (10¾ ounces each) cream of mushroom or cream of
    celery soup
2½ cups milk or water
½ pound ham, cubed
⅓ cup shredded colby cheese (optional)

• Cook cauliflower according to package directions; drain.

• Combine cauliflower, soup, milk and ham in saucepan; mix well.

• Cook over medium heat 4 to 6 minutes, stirring occasionally. Top individual servings with cheese.   *Makes 4 to 6 servings*

Prep Time: 2 minutes
Cook Time: 10 to 12 minutes

Potato & Spinach Soup with Gouda

9 medium Yukon Gold potatoes, peeled and cubed (about 6 cups)
2 cans (14 ounces each) chicken broth
½ cup water
1 small red onion, finely chopped
5 ounces baby spinach leaves
½ teaspoon salt
¼ teaspoon ground red pepper
¼ teaspoon black pepper
2½ cups shredded smoked Gouda cheese, divided
1 can (12 ounces) evaporated milk
1 tablespoon olive oil
4 cloves garlic, cut into thin slices
5 to 7 sprigs parsley, finely chopped

Slow Cooker Directions

1. Combine potatoes, chicken broth, water, onion, spinach, salt, red and black pepper in 4-quart slow cooker. Cover; cook on LOW 10 hours or until potatoes are tender.

2. Slightly mash potatoes in slow cooker; add 2 cups Gouda and evaporated milk. Cover; cook on HIGH 15 to 20 minutes or until cheese is melted.

3. Heat oil in small skillet over low heat. Cook and stir garlic 2 minutes or until golden brown; set aside. Pour soup into bowls. Sprinkle 2 to 3 teaspoons remaining Gouda cheese in each bowl. Add spoonful of garlic to center of each bowl; sprinkle with parsley.

Makes 8 to 10 servings

Serving Suggestion: This soup goes well with simple fish dinners, or you can add ham and serve it as an entire meal. If you add ham, eliminate the salt in the recipe.

Fish & Seafood

Smoked Salmon Hash Browns

3 cups frozen hash brown potatoes, thawed
2 pouches (3 ounces each) smoked salmon*
½ cup chopped onion
½ cup chopped bell pepper
¼ teaspoon black pepper
2 tablespoons vegetable oil

Smoked salmon in foil pouches can be found in the canned fish section of the supermarket. Do not substitute lox or other fresh smoked salmon.

1. Combine potatoes, salmon, onion, bell pepper and black pepper in bowl; toss gently to mix well.

2. Heat oil in large nonstick skillet over medium-high heat. Add potato mixture; spread to cover surface of skillet. Carefully pat down to avoid oil spatter.

3. Cook 5 minutes or until crisp and browned. Turn over in large pieces. Cook 2 to 3 minutes or until brown on both sides.

Makes 4 servings

Smoked Salmon Hash
Browns

Cheesy Tuna Pie

2 cups cooked rice
2 cans (6 ounces each) tuna, drained and flaked
1 cup mayonnaise
1 cup (4 ounces) shredded Cheddar cheese
1 can (4 ounces) sliced black olives
½ cup thinly sliced celery
½ cup sour cream
2 tablespoons dried onion flakes
1 refrigerated pie crust dough

1. Preheat oven to 350°F. Spray 9-inch deep-dish pie plate with nonstick cooking spray.

2. Combine rice, tuna, mayonnaise, cheese, olives, celery, sour cream and onion flakes in medium bowl; mix well. Spoon into prepared pie plate. Place pie dough over tuna mixture; press edge to pan to seal. Cut slits for steam to escape.

3. Bake 20 minutes or until crust is browned and filling is bubbly.

Makes 6 servings

Note: This recipe is great because it's simple and uses ingredients that you probably have on hand. Serve with a tossed green salad for a complete meal.

Fish with Hidden Valley Ranch®
Tartar Sauce

  1 cup (½ pint) sour cream
  ¼ cup chopped sweet pickles
  1 packet (1 ounce) HIDDEN VALLEY® The Original Ranch®
     Salad Dressing & Seasoning Mix
  ¾ cup dry bread crumbs
1½ pounds white fish fillets (sole, flounder, snapper or turbot)
  1 egg, beaten
    Vegetable oil
    French fried shoestring potatoes (optional)
    Lemon wedges (optional)

To make sauce, in small bowl, combine sour cream, pickles and
2 tablespoons of the salad dressing & seasoning mix; cover and
refrigerate. On large plate, combine bread crumbs and remaining
salad dressing mix. Dip fillets in egg, then coat with bread crumb
mixture. Fry fillets in 3 tablespoons oil until golden. (Add more oil to
pan if necessary to prevent sticking.) Serve with chilled sauce. Serve
with lemon wedges, if desired. *Makes 4 servings*

may the road rise to meet you

Hazelnut-Coated Salmon Steaks

¼ cup hazelnuts
4 salmon steaks (about 5 ounces each)
1 tablespoon apple butter
1 tablespoon Dijon mustard
¼ teaspoon dried thyme
⅛ teaspoon black pepper

1. Preheat oven to 375°F. Place hazelnuts on baking sheet; bake 8 minutes or until lightly browned. Quickly transfer nuts to clean dry dish towel. Fold towel over nuts; rub vigorously to remove as much of skins as possible. Using food processor, finely chop hazelnuts.

2. *Increase oven temperature to 450°F.* Place salmon in single layer in lightly greased baking dish. Combine apple butter, mustard, thyme and pepper in small bowl. Brush onto salmon; top each steak with hazelnuts, pressing lightly. Bake 14 to 16 minutes or until salmon flakes easily when tested with fork. Serve with herbed rice and steamed sugar snap peas, if desired. *Makes 4 servings*

Baked Cod with Tomatoes and Olives

1 pound cod fillets (about 4 fillets), cut into 2-inch pieces
   Salt and black pepper
1 can (14½ ounces) diced Italian-style tomatoes, drained
2 tablespoons chopped pitted ripe olives
1 teaspoon minced garlic
2 tablespoons chopped fresh parsley

1. Preheat oven to 400°F. Spray 13×9-inch baking dish with nonstick olive oil-flavored cooking spray. Arrange cod fillets in prepared dish; season with salt and pepper.

2. Combine tomatoes, olives and garlic in medium bowl. Spoon over fish.

3. Bake 20 minutes or until fish flakes when tested with fork. Sprinkle with parsley. *Makes 4 servings*

Prep and Cook Time: 25 minutes

Hazelnut-Coated
Salmon Steak

Elegant Shrimp Scampi

¼ cup (½ stick) plus 2 tablespoons butter
6 to 8 large cloves garlic, minced
1½ pounds large raw shrimp (about 16), peeled and deveined
6 green onions, thinly sliced
¼ cup dry white wine
    Juice of 1 lemon (about 2 tablespoons)
¼ cup chopped fresh parsley
    Salt and black pepper to taste
    Lemon slices and fresh parsley sprigs (optional)

1. Clarify butter by melting it in small saucepan over low heat. *Do not stir.* Skim off the white foam that forms on top. Strain clarified butter through cheesecloth into glass measuring cup to yield ⅓ cup. Discard milky residue at bottom of pan.

2. Heat clarified butter in large skillet over medium heat. Add garlic; cook and stir 1 to 2 minutes until softened but not brown.

3. Add shrimp, green onions, wine and lemon juice. Cook and stir 1 to 2 minutes on each side or until shrimp turn pink and are firm and opaque. Do not overcook.

4. Just before serving, add chopped parsley and season with salt and pepper. Serve on individual shell-shaped or small gratin dishes. Garnish with lemon slices and parsley sprigs.

Makes 8 appetizer servings

Smoked Salmon Roses

1 package (8 ounces) cream cheese, softened
1 tablespoon prepared horseradish
1 tablespoon minced fresh dill plus whole sprigs
1 tablespoon half-and-half
16 slices (12 to 16 ounces) smoked salmon
1 red bell pepper, cut into thin strips

1. Combine cream cheese, horseradish, minced dill and half-and-half in small bowl. Beat until light and creamy.

2. Spread 1 tablespoon cream cheese mixture over each salmon slice. Roll up jelly-roll fashion. Slice each roll in half crosswise. Arrange salmon rolls, cut sides down, on serving dish to resemble roses. Garnish each "rose" by tucking 1 pepper strip and 1 dill sprig into center. *Makes 32 servings*

Buttery Pepper and Citrus Broiled Fish

3 tablespoons MOLLY MCBUTTER® Flavored Sprinkles
1 tablespoon MRS. DASH® Lemon Pepper Blend
1 tablespoon lime juice
2 teaspoons honey
1 pound boneless white fish fillets

Combine first 4 ingredients in small bowl; mix well. Broil fish 6 to 8 inches from heat, turning once. Spread with Lemon Pepper mixture. Broil an additional 4 to 5 minutes. *Makes 4 servings*

Prep Time: 5 minutes
Cook Time: 10 minutes

Smoked Salmon Roses

Speedy Salmon Patties

1 can (12 ounces) pink salmon, undrained
¼ cup minced green onions
1 egg, lightly beaten
1 tablespoon chopped fresh dill
1 clove garlic, minced
½ cup all-purpose flour
1½ teaspoons baking powder
1½ cups vegetable oil

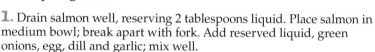

1. Drain salmon well, reserving 2 tablespoons liquid. Place salmon in medium bowl; break apart with fork. Add reserved liquid, green onions, egg, dill and garlic; mix well.

2. Combine flour and baking powder in small bowl; add to salmon mixture. Stir until well blended. Shape mixture into 6 patties.

3. Heat oil in large skillet to 350°F. Add salmon patties; cook until golden brown on both sides. Remove from oil; drain on paper towels. Serve warm.

Makes 6 patties

Oysters Romano

12 oysters, shucked and on the half shell
2 slices bacon, cut into 12 (1-inch) pieces
½ cup Italian-seasoned dry bread crumbs
2 tablespoons butter or margarine, melted
½ teaspoon garlic salt
6 tablespoons grated Romano, Parmesan or provolone cheese
Fresh chives (optional)

1. Preheat oven to 375°F. Place oysters in shells on baking sheet. Top each oyster with 1 piece bacon. Bake 10 minutes or until bacon is crisp.

2. Meanwhile, combine bread crumbs, butter and garlic salt in small bowl. Spoon mixture over oysters; top with cheese. Bake 5 to 10 minutes or until cheese melts. Garnish with chives, if desired.

Makes 4 appetizer servings

Trout with Apples and Toasted Hazelnuts

⅓ cup whole hazelnuts
5 tablespoons butter or margarine, divided
1 large Red Delicious apple, cored and cut into 16 wedges
2 butterflied rainbow trout fillets (about 8 ounces each)
   Salt and black pepper
3 tablespoons all-purpose flour
1 tablespoon lemon juice
1 tablespoon snipped fresh chives
   Lemon slices and fresh chives (optional)

1. Preheat oven to 375°F. Place hazelnuts on baking sheet; bake 8 minutes or until lightly browned. Quickly transfer nuts to clean dry dish towel. Fold towel over nuts; rub vigorously to remove as much of skins as possible. Using food processor, finely chop hazelnuts.

2. Melt 3 tablespoons butter in medium skillet over medium-high heat. Add apple; cook 4 to 5 minutes or until crisp-tender. Remove from skillet with slotted spoon; set aside.

3. Rinse trout and pat dry with paper towels. Sprinkle fish with salt and pepper, then coat in flour. Place fish in skillet. Cook 4 minutes or until golden and fish flakes easily when tested with fork, turning halfway through cooking time. Return apple to skillet. Reduce heat to low and keep warm.

4. Melt remaining 2 tablespoons butter in small saucepan over low heat. Stir in lemon juice, chives and hazelnuts. To serve, sprinkle fish and apple with hazelnut mixture. Garnish with lemon slices and chives. *Makes 2 servings*

Trout with Apples and
Toasted Hazelnuts

Meat & Poultry

Chicken with Kale Stuffing

4 boneless skinless chicken breasts
1 cup sliced mushrooms
½ cup chopped onion
2 tablespoons dry white wine
1 teaspoon chopped fresh oregano *or* ¼ teaspoon dried oregano
1 clove garlic, minced
½ teaspoon black pepper
2 cups chopped stemmed washed kale
2 tablespoons light mayonnaise
½ cup seasoned bread crumbs

1. Preheat oven to 400°F. Coat shallow baking dish with nonstick cooking spray; set aside. Remove fat from chicken. Pound chicken with meat mallet to ½-inch thickness; set aside.

2. Heat skillet over medium-high heat. Add mushrooms, onion, wine, oregano, garlic and pepper; cook and stir about 5 minutes or until onion is softened. Add kale; cook and stir until kale is wilted.

3. Spread kale mixture evenly over flattened chicken breasts. Roll up chicken; secure with toothpicks or metal skewers. Brush chicken with mayonnaise; coat with bread crumbs. Place chicken, seam side down, in prepared baking dish. Bake 25 minutes or until bread crumbs are golden brown and chicken is cooked through. Remove toothpicks before serving.   *Makes 4 servings*

Chicken with Kale Stuffing

Corned Beef and Cabbage

1 head cabbage (1½ pounds), cut into 6 wedges
4 ounces baby carrots
1 corned beef (3 pounds) with seasoning packet*
1 quart (4 cups) water
⅓ cup prepared mustard
⅓ cup honey

If seasoning packet is not perforated, poke several small holes with tip of paring knife.

Slow Cooker Directions

1. Place cabbage in slow cooker; top with carrots. Place seasoning packet on top of vegetables. Place corned beef, fat side up, over seasoning packet and vegetables. Add water. Cover; cook on LOW 10 hours. Discard seasoning packet.

2. Combine mustard and honey in small bowl. Slice beef and serve with vegetables and mustard sauce. *Makes 6 servings*

Shepherd's Pie

1⅓ cups instant mashed potato flakes
1⅔ cups milk
2 tablespoons margarine or butter
1 teaspoon salt, divided
1 pound ground beef
¼ teaspoon black pepper
1 jar (12 ounces) beef gravy
1 package (10 ounces) frozen mixed vegetables, thawed and drained
¾ cup grated Parmesan cheese

1. Preheat broiler. Prepare 4 servings of mashed potatoes according to package directions, using milk, margarine and ½ teaspoon salt.

2. Meanwhile, brown beef in large broilerproof skillet over medium-high heat, stirring to break up meat. Drain fat. Sprinkle beef with remaining ½ teaspoon salt and pepper. Add gravy and vegetables; mix well. Cook over medium-low heat 5 minutes or until hot.

3. Spoon prepared potatoes around outside edge of skillet, leaving 3-inch circle in center. Sprinkle cheese evenly over potatoes. Broil 4 to 5 inches from heat 3 minutes or until cheese is golden brown and beef mixture is bubbly. *Makes 4 servings*

Roast Pork Chops with Apple and Cabbage

3 teaspoons olive oil, divided
½ medium onion, thinly sliced
1 teaspoon dried thyme
2 cloves garlic, minced
4 pork chops (6 to 8 ounces each), 1 inch thick
Salt
¼ teaspoon black pepper, plus additional to taste
¼ cup cider vinegar
1 tablespoon packed brown sugar
1 large McIntosh apple, chopped
½ (8-ounce) package shredded coleslaw mix

1. Preheat oven to 375°F.

2. Heat 2 teaspoons oil in large ovenproof skillet over medium-high heat until hot. Add onion; cook, covered, 4 to 6 minutes or until tender, stirring often. Add thyme and garlic; cook and stir 30 seconds. Transfer to small bowl; set aside.

3. Add remaining 1 teaspoon oil to same skillet. Season pork chops with salt and pepper. Place in skillet; cook 2 minutes on each side or until browned. Remove pork chops from skillet; set aside.

4. Remove skillet from heat. Add vinegar, brown sugar and ¼ teaspoon pepper; stir to dissolve sugar and scrape cooked bits from skillet. Add onion mixture, apple and coleslaw mix; do not stir.

5. Arrange pork chops on top of cabbage mixture, overlapping to fit. Cover pan; place in oven. Bake 15 minutes or until pork chops are juicy and just barely pink in center. *Makes 4 servings*

Prep and Cook Time: 35 minutes

Harvest Pot Roast with Sweet Potatoes

   1 envelope LIPTON® RECIPE SECRETS® Onion Soup Mix
1½ cups water
   ¼ cup soy sauce
   2 tablespoons firmly packed dark brown sugar
   1 teaspoon ground ginger (optional)
   1 (3- to 3½-pound) boneless pot roast (rump, chuck or round)
   4 large sweet potatoes, peeled, if desired, and cut into large chunks
   3 tablespoons water
   2 tablespoons all-purpose flour

1. Preheat oven to 325°F. In Dutch oven or 5-quart heavy ovenproof saucepot, combine soup mix, water, soy sauce, brown sugar and ginger; add roast.

2. Cover and bake 1 hour 45 minutes.

3. Add potatoes and bake covered an additional 45 minutes or until beef and potatoes are tender.

4. Remove roast and potatoes to serving platter and keep warm; reserve juices.

5. In small cup, with wire whisk, blend water and flour. In same Dutch oven, add flour mixture to reserved juices. Bring to a boil over high heat. Boil, stirring occasionally, 2 minutes. Serve with roast and potatoes.
Makes 6 servings

Harvest Pot Roast with
Sweet Potatoes

Lemon-Rosemary Roasted Chicken

1 (6- to 7-pound) chicken, rinsed inside and out, and patted dry
1 teaspoon olive oil, divided
1 teaspoon salt, divided
¼ teaspoon black pepper
2 lemons
2½ teaspoons chopped dried rosemary *or* 2 (4-inch) sprigs fresh
    rosemary, chopped, divided
2 teaspoons butter, softened
1 large onion, cut in ½-inch slices
¾ cup chicken broth
½ teaspoon ground sage

1. Preheat oven to 450°F. Rub chicken with ½ teaspoon oil. Season with ½ teaspoon salt and pepper. Grate 2 teaspoons peel from one lemon; reserve.

2. Pierce same lemon in several places with knife tip or fork; place in chicken's cavity. Mix 2 teaspoons rosemary and butter to blend. Carefully loosen skin on breast. Gently smooth butter mixture under the skin. Tie legs with kitchen string, if desired.

3. Place onion slices in middle of roasting pan and put chicken on top. Roast 45 minutes, then tent breast with foil. Continue roasting 30 to 40 minutes longer or until internal temperature reaches 170°F and chicken is golden brown. Baste with pan drippings every 30 minutes.

4. Transfer chicken to cutting board; let rest 10 minutes. Pour pan drippings into liquid measuring cup and remove fat. Squeeze 1 teaspoon juice from second lemon; add to drippings.

5. Return drippings to roasting pan, or transfer drippings to medium skillet; add any drippings from chicken. Add reserved peel, remaining ½ teaspoon salt, remaining ½ teaspoon rosemary, broth and sage; simmer on medium-high heat. Scrape up browned bits; continue simmering until gravy cooks down to 1 cup. Carve chicken and serve with gravy. *Makes 8 to 10 servings*

Cook's Tip: Using thick onion slices as a "rack" on which to set the chicken imparts flavor to the drippings. Cleanup is much easier, as well.

Lemon-Rosemary Roasted
Chicken

Warm Australian Lamb Salad with Sweet Potato

1 leg of Australian Lamb, butterflied (see tip)
   Sea salt, to taste
   Freshly ground pepper, to taste

Salad and Dressing
   2 pounds sweet potatoes (2 large or 3 medium)
   2 tablespoons olive oil
   2 bunches arugula, torn
   1 small red onion, halved and thinly sliced
   ⅓ cup extra-virgin olive oil
   2 tablespoons red wine or sherry vinegar
   Juice and zest of ½ orange
   Salt and freshly ground pepper, to taste
   6 ounces of feta cheese, crumbled

1. Trim lamb and season with salt and pepper.

2. Preheat oven to 375° F. Peel and dice the potatoes into ½-inch pieces and toss with the olive oil to coat. Place on a baking sheet and cook for 20 to 30 minutes, or until tender and golden brown.

3. Heat grill or grill pan to medium-high and cook lamb for 5 minutes on each side. Cover barbecue or transfer lamb to the oven and cook for 8 to 10 minutes or until medium rare and internal temperature reaches 125 to 130°F. Cover loosely with foil and allow to rest for 15 minutes.

4. To finish the salad, while lamb is resting, whisk the dressing ingredients together and season to taste. Toss the arugula, onion and warm potatoes together in a bowl, add half the dressing and mix well. Place on a platter or individual plates. Slice lamb thinly across the grain and arrange over the salad. Scatter with the feta cheese and drizzle with remaining dressing. *Makes 6 servings*

Tip: To butterfly the lamb, remove netting and open out the leg to make as flat as possible. Pound to desired thinness.

Favorite recipe from **Meat and Livestock Australia**

Warm Australian Lamb
Salad with Sweet Potato

Onion-Apple Glazed Pork Tenderloin

1 (1½- to 2-pound) boneless pork tenderloin
  Ground black pepper
2 tablespoons BERTOLLI® Olive Oil, divided
1 envelope LIPTON® RECIPE SECRETS® Onion Soup Mix
½ cup apple juice
2 tablespoons firmly packed brown sugar
¾ cup water
¼ cup dry red wine or water
1 tablespoon all-purpose flour

1. Preheat oven to 425°F. In small roasting pan or baking pan, arrange pork. Season with pepper and rub with 1 tablespoon olive oil. Roast uncovered 10 minutes.

2. Meanwhile, in small bowl, combine remaining 1 tablespoon olive oil, soup mix, apple juice and brown sugar. Pour over pork and continue roasting 10 minutes or until desired doneness. Remove pork to serving platter; cover with aluminum foil.

3. Place roasting pan over medium-high heat and bring pan juices to a boil, scraping up any browned bits from bottom of pan. Stir in water, wine and flour; boil, stirring constantly, 1 minute or until thickened.

4. To serve, thinly slice pork and serve with gravy.

Makes 4 to 6 servings

Prep Time: 5 minutes
Cook Time: 25 minutes

Delicious Lamb Kabobs

½ cup apple juice

2 tablespoons Worcestershire sauce, divided

2 tablespoons oil

1 teaspoon lemon pepper

2 cloves garlic, minced

1½ pounds boneless lamb leg, cut into 1¼-inch cubes

1 cup chili sauce

½ cup apple jelly or orange marmalade

1 teaspoon Dijon mustard

¼ teaspoon red pepper flakes

2 medium onions, cut into wedges

2 medium apples, cut into wedges

2 green bell peppers, cut into wedges

1. Combine apple juice, 1 tablespoon Worcestershire sauce, oil, lemon pepper and garlic in large resealable food storage bag or nonmetal container. Add lamb cubes; coat well. Marinate in refrigerator 2 to 24 hours.

2. Combine chili sauce, jelly, remaining 1 tablespoon Worcestershire sauce, mustard and red pepper flakes in medium saucepan. Simmer 10 to 15 minutes, stirring occasionally, until slightly thickened.

3. Preheat grill or broiler. Remove meat from marinade; discard marinade. Thread onto skewers, alternating meat, vegetables and apples. (If using bamboo skewers, soak in water for 20 to 30 minutes before using to prevent them from burning.)

4. To grill, place kabobs 4 inches from medium coals. Cook 10 to 12 minutes, turning occasionally and brushing with chili sauce mixture. To broil, place kabobs on broiler pan sprayed with nonstick cooking spray. Broil 4 inches from heat about 10 to 12 minutes for medium-rare, turning occasionally and brushing with chili sauce mixture. *Makes 6 servings*

Old-Fashioned Cabbage Rolls

½ **pound ground beef**
½ **pound ground veal**
½ **pound ground pork**
1 **small onion, chopped**
2 **eggs, lightly beaten**
½ **cup dry bread crumbs**
1 **teaspoon salt**
1 **teaspoon molasses**
¼ **teaspoon ground ginger**
¼ **teaspoon ground nutmeg**
¼ **teaspoon ground allspice**
1 **large head cabbage, separated into leaves**
3 **cups boiling water**
¼ **cup butter**
½ **cup milk, plus additional if necessary**
1 **tablespoon cornstarch**

1. Combine meats and onion in large bowl. Combine eggs, bread crumbs, salt, molasses, ginger, nutmeg and allspice in medium bowl; mix well. Add to meat mixture; stir until well blended.

2. Drop cabbage leaves into boiling water for 3 minutes. Remove with slotted spoon, reserving ½ cup of boiling liquid.

3. Preheat oven to 375°F. Place about 2 tablespoons meat mixture about 1 inch from stem end of each cabbage leaf. Fold sides in and roll up, fastening with toothpicks, if necessary.

4. Heat butter in large skillet over medium-high heat. Add cabbage rolls, 3 or 4 at a time, to skillet and brown on all sides. Arrange rolls, seam side down, in single layer in casserole. Combine reserved boiling liquid with butter remaining in skillet; pour over cabbage rolls.

5. Bake 1 hour. Carefully drain accumulated pan juices into measuring cup. Return cabbage rolls to oven.

6. Add enough milk to reserved pan juices to equal 1 cup. Pour milk mixture into small saucepan. Stir in cornstarch; bring to a boil, stirring constantly until sauce is thickened. Pour over cabbage rolls. Bake 15 minutes more or until sauce is browned and cabbage is tender.

Makes 8 servings

Beef with Apples & Sweet Potatoes

1 boneless beef chuck shoulder roast (2 pounds)
1 can (40 ounces) sweet potatoes, drained
2 small onions, sliced
2 apples, cored and sliced
½ cup beef broth
2 cloves garlic, minced
1 teaspoon salt
1 teaspoon dried thyme, divided
¾ teaspoon black pepper, divided
1 tablespoon cornstarch
¼ teaspoon ground cinnamon
2 tablespoons cold water

Slow Cooker Directions

1. Trim and discard fat from beef. Cut beef into 2-inch pieces. Place beef, sweet potatoes, onions, apples, beef broth, garlic, salt, ½ teaspoon thyme and ½ teaspoon pepper in 4-quart slow cooker. Cover; cook on LOW 8 to 9 hours.

2. Transfer beef, sweet potatoes and apples to platter; keep warm. Let liquid stand 5 minutes to allow fat to rise. Skim off and discard fat.

3. Stir together cornstarch, remaining ½ teaspoon thyme, ¼ teaspoon pepper, cinnamon and water until smooth; stir into cooking liquid. Cook 15 minutes on HIGH or until juices are thickened. Serve sauce over beef, sweet potatoes and apples. *Makes 6 servings*

Prep Time: 20 minutes
Cook Time: 8 to 9 hours

Beef with Apples & Sweet
Potatoes

Sides & Gravies

Sweet-Sour Cabbage with Apples and Caraway Seeds

4 cups shredded red cabbage

1 large tart apple, peeled, quartered, cored and cut crosswise into ¼-inch-thick slices

¼ cup packed light brown sugar

¼ cup cider vinegar

¼ cup water

½ teaspoon salt

¼ teaspoon caraway seeds

Dash black pepper

1. Combine cabbage, apple, brown sugar, vinegar, water, salt, caraway seeds and pepper in large saucepan. Cook, covered, over medium heat 10 minutes. Stir mixture.

2. Cook, covered, over medium-low heat 15 to 20 minutes or until cabbage is crisp-tender and apple is tender. Serve warm or chilled.

Makes 6 servings

Sweet-Sour Cabbage with Apples and Caraway Seeds

Rustic Cheddar Mashed Potatoes

2 pounds russet potatoes, peeled and diced
1 cup water
⅓ cup butter, cut into small pieces
½ to ¾ cup milk
1¼ teaspoons salt
½ teaspoon black pepper
½ cup finely chopped green onions
¾ cup (3 ounces) shredded Cheddar cheese

Slow Cooker Directions

1. Combine potatoes and water in slow cooker; dot with butter. Cover; cook on LOW 6 hours or on HIGH 3 hours or until potatoes are tender. Remove potatoes to large mixing bowl.

2. Whip potatoes with electric mixer at medium speed until well blended. Add milk, salt and pepper; whip until smooth.

3. Stir in green onions and cheese; cover. Let stand 15 minutes to allow flavors to blend and cheese to melt. *Makes 8 servings*

Mushroom Gravy

1 tablespoon butter or margarine
1 cup sliced mushrooms
2 cups water
4 teaspoons HERB-OX® beef flavored bouillon
¼ cup all purpose flour
    Salt and pepper, to taste

In large skillet, over medium-high heat, in butter, sauté mushrooms about 3 to 5 minutes or until golden brown and slightly softened. Add water and bouillon. Gradually add flour to saucepan; whisking until smooth. Cook and stir over medium heat till thickened and bubbly. Cook and stir for 1 minute more. Season to taste with salt and pepper.
Makes about 2 cups

Prep Time: 5 minutes
Total Time: 15 minutes

Rustic Cheddar Mashed
Potatoes

Steamed Broccoli & Carrots

1 pound broccoli
12 baby carrots*
1 tablespoon butter
Salt and black pepper

*Substitute ½ pound regular carrots, cut into 2-inch chunks for baby carrots.

1. Break broccoli into florets. Discard large stems. Trim smaller stems; cut into thin slices.

2. Place 2 to 3 inches of water and steamer basket in large saucepan; bring water to a boil.

3. Add broccoli and carrots; cover. Steam 6 minutes or until vegetables are crisp-tender.

4. Place vegetables in serving bowl. Add butter; toss lightly to coat. Season to taste with salt and pepper.   *Makes 4 servings*

Stone Ground Mustard Mashed Potatoes

2½ pounds potatoes
½ cup cream
¼ cup butter
¼ cup PLOCHMAN'S ® Stone Ground Mustard

Peel, cut up, and boil potatoes until tender. Drain and mash. Bring cream and butter to a boil, add to potatoes and mix in thoroughly. Mix in mustard and serve hot.   *Makes 6 servings*

Sláinte!

Potato-Cabbage Pancakes

½ cup refrigerated shredded hash brown potatoes
½ cup coleslaw mix, lightly packed
¼ cup egg whites
¼ teaspoon white pepper
4 tablespoons unsweetened applesauce (optional)
2 tablespoons sour cream (optional)

1. Mix potatoes, slaw, egg whites and pepper in medium bowl.

2. Spray large nonstick skillet with nonstick cooking spray and heat over medium-high.

3. Scoop batter into ¼-cup measure. Gently invert cup into skillet. Repeat with second pancake. Drizzle any juices from bowl over pancakes.

4. When batter begins to sizzle, gently press down with spatula to flatten into pancakes that are ½ inch thick and about 2 inches in diameter. Cook about 4 minutes until pancake browns on one side. Turn pancakes. Cook 4 minutes on second side until pancake browns.

5. Serve each pancake with applesauce or sour cream, if desired.

Makes 2 servings

Steamed Kale

3 pounds fresh kale
3 tablespoons butter or margarine, divided
6 tablespoons water, divided

1. Rinse kale well in large bowl of cold water. Place in colander; drain.

2. Discard any discolored leaves. To trim away tough stems, make "V-shaped" cut at stem end; discard tough stems. Stack leaves and cut into 3- to 4-inch pieces.

3. Melt 1 tablespoon butter with 2 tablespoons water in Dutch oven over medium-high heat. Add about one-third of kale; cook and stir 1 minute. Cover Dutch oven and steam kale 3 to 5 minutes or until kale is wilted and tender but not soft, stirring occasionally.

4. Transfer to large bowl; cover to keep warm. Steam remaining kale in two batches using 1 tablespoon butter and 2 tablespoons water for each batch.

Makes about 5 cups

Potato-Cabbage Pancakes

Roast Herbed Sweet Potatoes with Bacon & Onions

3 thick slices applewood-smoked bacon or peppered bacon, diced
2 pounds sweet potatoes, peeled and cut into 2-inch chunks
2 medium onions, cut into 8 wedges
1 teaspoon salt
1 teaspoon dried thyme
¼ teaspoon black pepper

1. Preheat oven to 375°F. Cook bacon in large, deep skillet over medium heat until crisp. Remove from heat. Transfer bacon to paper towels; set aside. Add potatoes and onions to drippings in skillet; toss until coated. Stir in salt, thyme and pepper.

2. Spread mixture in single layer in ungreased 15×10-inch jelly-roll pan or shallow roasting pan. Bake 40 to 50 minutes or until golden brown and sweet potatoes are tender. Transfer to serving bowl; sprinkle with bacon. *Makes 10 to 12 servings*

Orange-Spice Glazed Carrots

1 pound fresh or thawed frozen baby carrots
⅓ cup orange marmalade
2 tablespoons butter
2 teaspoons Dijon mustard
½ teaspoon grated fresh ginger

Heat 1 inch lightly salted water in 2-quart saucepan over high heat to a boil; add carrots. Return to a boil. Reduce heat to low. Cover and simmer 10 to 12 minutes for fresh carrots (8 to 10 minutes for frozen carrots) or until crisp-tender. Drain well; return carrots to pan. Stir in marmalade, butter, mustard and ginger. Simmer, uncovered, over medium heat 3 minutes or until carrots are glazed, stirring occasionally.* *Makes 6 servings*

At this point, carrots may be transferred to a microwavable casserole dish with lid. Cover and refrigerate up to 8 hours before serving. To reheat, microwave on HIGH (100% power) 4 to 5 minutes or until hot.

Roast Herbed Sweet Potatoes
with Bacon & Onions

Cauliflower with Onion Butter

1 cup (2 sticks) butter, divided
1 cup diced onion
1 head cauliflower, cut into 2½×2-inch florets

1. Melt ½ cup butter in 10-inch skillet over medium heat. Cook onion, stirring occasionally, until brown (about 20 minutes).

2. Meanwhile, place cauliflower in microwavable container with ½ cup water. Cover and microwave on HIGH 8 minutes or until crisp-tender.

3. Add remaining butter to skillet with onions; cook, stirring frequently, until melted and well blended. Pour over cooked cauliflower and serve immediately. *Makes about 10 servings*

Yorkshire Pudding

2 eggs
1 cup flour
½ teaspoon salt
¾ cup milk
1¾ cups water, divided
1 package (1 ounces) LAWRY'S® Au Jus Gravy Mix
½ cup Port wine
Dash LAWRY'S® Seasoned Pepper
Vegetable oil

In medium bowl, using electric beater, beat eggs until frothy. Reduce speed and gradually add flour and salt, beat until smooth. Slowly add milk and ¼ cup of water, beat until well mixed. Increase speed to high and continue beating 10 minutes. Let stand 1 hour. In medium saucepan, prepare Au Jus Gravy Mix with 1½ cups water, wine and Seasoned Pepper according to package directions. Set aside. Preheat oven to 400°F. Coat 5-inch oven-safe omelet pan with oil and place in oven. When pan is very hot, remove and pour off excess oil. In pan, place 1 tablespoon Au Jus Gravy and ½ cup batter. Bake 20 to 30 minutes until puffed and brown. Remove and wrap in foil. Repeat until all batter has been used. *Makes 4 Yorkshire Puddings (8 servings)*

Meal Idea: Serve with prime rib or roast beef and remaining Au Jus Gravy.

Cauliflower with Onion
Butter

Oven "Chips"

2 small baking potatoes (10 ounces)
2 teaspoons olive oil
¼ teaspoon salt or onion salt

1. Place potatoes in refrigerator for 1 to 2 days.

2. Preheat oven to 450°F. Peel potatoes and cut lengthwise into
¼-inch square strips. Place in colander. Rinse potato strips under cold
running water 2 minutes. Drain. Pat dry with paper towels. Place
potatoes in small resealable food storage bag. Drizzle with oil. Seal
bag; shake to coat potatoes with oil.

3. Arrange potatoes in single layer on baking sheet. Bake 20 to
25 minutes or until light brown and crisp. Sprinkle with salt or onion
salt.   *Makes 2 servings*

Note: Refrigerating potatoes—usually not recommended—converts
starch in the potatoes to sugar, which enhances the browning when
the potatoes are baked. Do not refrigerate the potatoes longer than
2 days, because they might begin to taste sweet.

Three Onion Gravy

1 tablespoon butter or margarine
¼ cup coarsely chopped yellow onion
¼ cup coarsely chopped red onion
2 cups water
4 teaspoons HERB-OX® beef flavored bouillon
¼ cup all-purpose flour
2 tablespoons sliced chives
Salt and pepper, to taste

In large skillet, over medium-high heat, in butter, sauté onions until
softened, about 3 minutes. Add water and bouillon. Gradually add
flour to saucepan; whisking until smooth. Cook and stir over medium
heat till thickened and bubbly. Cook and stir for 1 minute more.
Season to taste with salt and pepper.   *Makes about 2½ cups*

Prep Time: 10 minutes
Total Time: 20 minutes

Breads

Irish Soda Bread

4 cups all-purpose flour
¼ cup sugar
1 tablespoon baking powder
1 teaspoon baking soda
1 teaspoon salt
1 tablespoon caraway seeds
⅓ cup shortening
1 cup raisins or currants
1 egg
1¾ cups buttermilk*

Soured fresh milk can be substituted for buttermilk. To sour milk, combine 2 tablespoons lemon juice plus enough milk to equal 1¾ cups. Stir; let stand 5 minutes before using.

1. Preheat oven to 350°F. Grease large baking sheet; set aside.

2. Sift flour, sugar, baking powder, baking soda and salt into large bowl. Stir in caraway seeds. Cut in shortening with pastry blender or two knives until mixture resembles coarse crumbs. Stir in raisins. Beat egg in medium bowl. Add buttermilk; beat until well blended. Add buttermilk mixture to flour mixture; stir until mixture forms soft dough that clings together and forms a ball.

3. Turn out dough onto well-floured surface. Knead dough gently 10 to 12 times. Place dough on prepared baking sheet. Pat dough into 7-inch round. Score top of dough with tip of sharp knife, making an "X" about 4 inches long and ¼ inch deep.

4. Bake 55 to 60 minutes or until toothpick inserted into center comes out clean. Immediately remove from baking sheet; cool on wire rack.** Bread is best eaten the day it is made.   *Makes 12 servings*

**For a sweet crust, combine 1 tablespoon sugar and 1 tablespoon water in small bowl; brush over hot loaf.*

Whole Wheat Popovers

1¼ cups whole wheat pastry flour*
1¼ cups milk
  3 eggs
  2 tablespoons melted butter
 ¼ teaspoon salt
  1 tablespoon cold butter, cut into 6 pieces

*Whole wheat pastry flour is available at natural food stores and some supermarkets. Half white pastry flour mixed with half whole wheat flour may be substituted.

1. Position rack in lower third of oven. Preheat oven to 400°F. Spray popover pan with nonstick cooking spray. (If popover pan is not available, jumbo muffin pans or custard cups may be used.)

2. Place flour, milk, eggs, melted butter and salt in food processor or blender. Process until batter is smooth and consistency of heavy cream. (Batter may also be blended in large bowl with electric mixer.) Meanwhile, place popover pan in oven for 2 minutes to preheat. Immediately place one piece of cold butter in each popover cup and return to oven 1 minute until butter melts.

3. Fill each cup halfway with batter. Bake 20 minutes. *Do not open oven or popovers may fall. Reduce oven temperature to 300°F. Bake 20 minutes more.* Remove from cups; cool slightly on wire rack. Serve warm. *Makes 6 popovers*

Cinnamon-Raisin Bread

½ cup plus 1 teaspoon sugar, divided
¼ cup warm water (105° to 115°F)
1 package (¼ ounce) active dry yeast
3 to 3½ cups all-purpose flour, divided
1 teaspoon salt
⅔ cup warm milk (105° to 115°F)
3 tablespoons butter, softened
1 whole egg
1 egg, separated
1 teaspoon vanilla
¾ cup raisins
1 tablespoon ground cinnamon
1 tablespoon butter or margarine, melted
1 tablespoon water

1. Combine 1 teaspoon sugar, warm water and yeast in small bowl; let stand 5 minutes or until bubbly.

2. Combine 1½ cups flour, ¼ cup sugar and salt in large bowl. Gradually beat yeast mixture, warm milk and softened butter into flour mixture with electric mixer at low speed until blended.

3. Beat in whole egg, egg yolk and vanilla on low speed. Increase speed to medium; beat 2 minutes. Add enough additional flour, about 1½ cups, to make soft dough.

4. Turn out onto lightly floured surface. Knead about 5 minutes adding enough of remaining flour to make a smooth and elastic dough. Knead in raisins. Dough will be soft and slightly sticky. Shape dough into a ball; place in large greased bowl. Turn dough over to grease top. Cover with towel; let rise in warm place 1 to 1½ hours or until doubled in bulk.

5. Punch down dough; knead on lightly floured surface 1 minute. Cover with towel; let rest 10 minutes. Grease 9×5-inch loaf pan; set aside. Combine remaining ¼ cup sugar and cinnamon in small bowl. Reserve 1 tablespoon mixture.

6. Roll dough into 20×9-inch rectangle with lightly floured rolling pin. Brush with 1 tablespoon melted butter. Sprinkle cinnamon mixture evenly over butter. Starting with 9-inch side, roll up dough jelly-roll style. Pinch ends and seam to seal. Place loaf, seam side down, in prepared pan, tucking ends under. Cover; let rise in warm place about 1¼ hours or until doubled in bulk. (Dough should rise to top of pan.)

continued on page 70

Cinnamon-Raisin Bread

7. Preheat oven to 350°F. Combine egg white and 1 tablespoon water in small bowl. Brush loaf with egg white mixture; sprinkle with reserved 1 tablespoon cinnamon mixture.

8. Bake 40 to 45 minutes or until loaf sounds hollow when tapped. Immediately remove from pan; cool completely on wire rack.

Makes 1 loaf

Rich Cranberry Scones

3 cups all-purpose flour
⅓ cup plus 1 tablespoon sugar, divided
1 tablespoon baking powder
½ teaspoon salt
½ cup I CAN'T BELIEVE IT'S NOT BUTTER!® Spread
¾ cup dried cranberries
1 cup plus 1 tablespoon whipping or heavy cream, divided
2 eggs

Preheat oven to 450°F.

In large bowl, combine flour, ⅓ cup sugar, baking powder and salt. With pastry blender or 2 knives, cut in I Can't Believe It's Not Butter!® Spread until mixture is size of fine crumbs. Stir in cranberries.

In small bowl, with wire whisk, blend 1 cup cream and eggs. Stir into flour mixture until dough forms. On floured surface, with floured hands, divide dough in half. Press each half into 6-inch circle. Cut each circle into 6 wedges; place on baking sheet. Brush with remaining 1 tablespoon cream, then sprinkle with remaining 1 tablespoon sugar.

Bake 12 minutes or until golden. Serve warm or cool completely on wire rack.

Makes 12 scones

Prep Time: 15 minutes
Cook Time: 12 minutes

Rich Cranberry Scones

Pull-Apart Rye Rolls

¾ cup water
2 tablespoons butter or margarine, softened
2 tablespoons molasses
2¼ cups all-purpose flour, divided
½ cup rye flour
⅓ cup nonfat dry milk powder
1 package (¼ ounce) active dry yeast
1½ teaspoons salt
1½ teaspoons caraway seeds
    Melted butter or vegetable oil

1. Heat water, 2 tablespoons butter and molasses in small saucepan over low heat until temperature reaches 120° to 130°F. Combine 1¼ cups all-purpose flour, rye flour, milk powder, yeast, salt and caraway seeds in large bowl. Stir heated water mixture into flour mixture with wooden spoon to form soft but sticky dough. Gradually add more all-purpose flour until rough dough forms.

2. Turn out dough onto lightly floured surface. Knead 5 to 8 minutes or until smooth and elastic, gradually adding remaining flour to prevent sticking, if necessary. Cover with inverted bowl. Let rise 35 to 40 minutes or until dough has increased in bulk by one third. Punch down dough; divide in half. Roll each half into 12-inch log. Using sharp knife, cut each log evenly into 12 pieces; shape into tight balls. Arrange in greased 8- or 9-inch cake pan. Brush tops with melted butter. Loosely cover with lightly greased sheet of plastic wrap. Let rise in warm place 45 minutes or until doubled in bulk.

3. Preheat oven to 375°F. Uncover rolls; bake 15 to 20 minutes or until golden brown. Cool in pan on wire rack 5 minutes. Remove from pan. Cool completely on wire rack. *Makes 24 rolls*

Pull-Apart Rye Rolls

Beer Batter Rye Bread

2 cups all-purpose flour
½ cup rye flour
2 tablespoons molasses or packed brown sugar
2 tablespoons vegetable oil
1 tablespoon caraway seeds
1 package (¼ ounce) active dry yeast
1 teaspoon salt
1 cup beer

1. Fit processor with steel blade. Measure 1 cup of the all-purpose flour, rye flour, molasses, oil, caraway seeds, yeast and salt into work bowl. Process until mixed, about 5 seconds.

2. Heat beer in small saucepan over low heat until 120° to 130°F. Turn on processor and add beer all at once through feed tube. Process until blended, about 30 seconds. Turn on processor and add remaining 1 cup flour, ¼ cup at a time, through feed tube. Process 5 to 10 seconds after each addition. (If food processor sounds strained and/or motor slows down or stops, turn off processor immediately and stir any remaining flour into batter by hand.)

3. Pour batter into greased 1½-quart baking dish. Let stand in warm place (85°F) about 45 minutes or until almost doubled in bulk.

4. Preheat oven to 350°F. Bake about 30 minutes or until toothpick inserted in center comes out clean. Cool 10 minutes. Remove bread from baking dish and cool on wire rack. *Makes 1 loaf*

Apple Sauce Irish Soda Bread

3 cups all-purpose flour
1 tablespoon sugar
2 teaspoons baking soda
1 teaspoon salt
1 cup low-fat buttermilk
½ cup MOTT'S® Natural Apple Sauce
2 tablespoons margarine, melted
½ cup raisins
2 tablespoons skim milk

1. Preheat oven to 375°F. Spray 8-inch round baking pan with nonstick cooking spray.

2. In large bowl, combine flour, sugar, baking soda and salt.

3. In small bowl, combine buttermilk, apple sauce and margarine.

4. Add apple sauce mixture to flour mixture; stir until mixture forms a ball.

5. Turn out dough onto well-floured surface; knead raisins into dough. Pat into 7-inch round.

6. Place dough in prepared pan. Cut cross in top of dough, ¼ inch deep, with tip of sharp knife. Brush top of dough with milk.

7. Bake 35 minutes or until toothpick inserted in center comes out clean. Cool in pan 10 minutes. Invert onto wire rack; turn right side up. Cool completely. Cut into 16 wedges. *Makes 16 servings*

Celtic Knots

1 package (16 ounces) hot roll mix, plus ingredients to prepare mix
1 egg white
2 teaspoons water
2 tablespoons coarse salt

1. Prepare hot roll mix according to package directions.

2. Preheat oven to 375°F. Lightly grease baking sheets.

3. Divide dough equally into 16 pieces; shape each piece into 10-inch rope. Form each rope into interlocking ring as shown in photo; place on prepared baking sheets. Moisten ends of rope at seams; pinch to seal.

4. Beat egg white and water in small bowl until foamy. Brush mixture onto dough; sprinkle with salt.

5. Bake about 15 minutes or until golden brown. Serve warm or at room temperature. *Makes 16 knots*

Pullaparts

1 package (11 ounces) refrigerated French bread dough
    Butter-flavored nonstick cooking spray
1 tablespoon olive oil
½ teaspoon dried basil (optional)
1 tablespoon grated Parmesan cheese

1. Preheat oven to 350°F.

2. Place dough roll on cutting board. Using a serrated knife, gently cut dough into 12 pieces.

3. Coat 9-inch round baking pan with cooking spray. Brush dough pieces lightly with oil. Arrange dough pieces, smooth side up, directly next to each other in pan. Sprinkle with basil, if desired. Bake 22 to 24 minutes or until golden and rolls sound hollow when gently tapped. Remove from oven to wire rack.

4. Lightly spray tops of rolls with cooking spray. Sprinkle with cheese. *Makes 12 servings*

Prep Time: 5 minutes
Bake Time: 23 minutes

Celtic Knots

Farmer-Style Sour Cream Bread

1 cup sour cream, at room temperature
3 tablespoons water
2½ to 3 cups all-purpose flour, divided
1 package active dry yeast
2 tablespoons sugar
1½ teaspoons salt
¼ teaspoon baking soda
Vegetable oil or nonstick cooking spray
1 tablespoon poppy or sesame seeds

1. Stir together sour cream and water in small saucepan. Heat over low heat until temperature reaches 120° to 130°F. *Do not boil.*

2. Combine 2 cups flour, yeast, sugar, salt and baking soda in large bowl. Spread sour cream mixture evenly over flour mixture with rubber spatula. Stir until well blended. Turn out dough onto lightly floured surface. Turn out onto lightly floured surface. Knead about 5 minutes adding enough of remaining flour to make a smooth and elastic dough.

3. Grease large baking sheet. Shape dough into ball; place on prepared sheet. Flatten into 8-inch circle. Brush top with oil. Sprinkle with poppy seeds. Invert large bowl over dough and let rise in warm place 1 hour or until doubled in bulk.

4. Preheat oven to 350°F. Bake 22 to 27 minutes or until golden brown. Remove immediately from baking sheet; cool on wire rack.

Makes 8 to 12 servings

Farmer-Style Sour
Cream Bread

Sweets

Toffee Bread Pudding with Cinnamon Toffee Sauce

  3 cups milk
  4 eggs
  ¾ cup sugar
  ¾ teaspoon ground cinnamon
  ¾ teaspoon vanilla extract
  ½ teaspoon salt
  6 to 6½ cups ½-inch cubes French, Italian or sourdough bread
  1 cup HEATH® BITS 'O BRICKLE® Toffee Bits, divided
    Cinnamon Toffee Sauce (recipe follows)
    Sweetened whipped cream or ice cream (optional)

1. Heat oven to 350°F. Butter 13×9×2-inch baking pan.

2. Mix together milk, eggs, sugar, cinnamon, vanilla and salt in large bowl with wire whisk. Stir in bread cubes, coating completely. Allow to stand 10 minutes. Stir in ½ cup toffee bits. Pour into prepared pan. Sprinkle remaining ½ cup toffee bits over surface.

3. Bake 40 to 45 minutes or until surface is set. Cool 30 minutes.

4. Meanwhile, prepare Cinnamon Toffee Sauce. Cut pudding into squares; top with sauce and sweetened whipped cream or ice cream, if desired. *Makes 12 servings*

Cinnamon Toffee Sauce: Combine ¾ cup HEATH® BITS 'O BRICKLE® Toffee Bits, ⅓ cup whipping cream and ⅛ teaspoon ground cinnamon in medium saucepan. Cook over low heat, stirring constantly, until toffee melts and mixture is well blended. (As toffee melts, small bits of almond will remain.) Makes about ⅔ cup sauce.

Note: This dessert is best eaten the same day it is prepared.

Toffee Bread Pudding with
Cinnamon Toffee Sauce

Brown Sugar Shortbread

1 cup (2 sticks) I CAN'T BELIEVE IT'S NOT BUTTER!® Spread
¾ cup firmly packed light brown sugar
2 cups all-purpose flour
⅓ cup semisweet chocolate chips, melted

Preheat oven to 325°F. Grease 9-inch round cake pan; set aside.

In large bowl, with electric mixer, beat I Can't Believe It's Not Butter!® Spread and brown sugar until light and fluffy, about 5 minutes. Gradually add flour and beat on low until blended. Spread mixture into prepared pan and press into even layer. With knife, score surface into 16 pie-shaped wedges.

Bake 45 minutes or until lightly golden. On wire rack, cool 20 minutes; remove from pan and cool completely. To serve, pour melted chocolate into small plastic storage bag. Snip corner and drizzle chocolate over shortbread. Cut into wedges.   *Makes 16 servings*

Irish Kisses

3 egg whites
½ teaspoon cream of tartar
Pinch of salt
¾ cup sugar
4 drops green food coloring
4 drops mint extract
1 package (6 ounces) miniature semisweet chocolate chips

1. Preheat oven to 375°F. Grease and lightly flour two cookie sheets.

2. Beat egg whites with cream of tartar and salt until foamy. Gradually beat in sugar, 2 tablespoons at a time; until soft peaks form. Stir in food coloring and mint extract. Fold in chocolate chips.

3. Drop meringue by teaspoonfuls, 1 inch apart, onto prepared cookie sheets. Place in preheated oven; close door. Turn off heat; let meringues set in oven 8 to 12 hours.   *Makes about 4 dozen cookies*

Spicy Apple Upside-Down Cake

Cake

- ½ cup (1 stick) butter, melted
- ¾ cup packed dark brown sugar
- 2 Braeburn apples, thinly sliced
- 1 package (about 18 ounces) carrot cake mix, plus ingredients to prepare mix

Sauce

- ½ cup (1 stick) butter
- ½ cup packed dark brown sugar
- ¼ cup whiskey

1. Preheat oven to 350°F. Lightly grease 9-inch springform pan. Wrap outside of pan tightly in heavy-duty foil.

2. For cake, pour melted butter into pan; tilt pan to spread butter evenly over bottom of pan. Sprinkle ¾ cup brown sugar evenly over butter. Arrange apple slices, overlapping slightly, in spiral pattern in pan.

3. Prepare cake mix according to package directions. Carefully spoon cake batter over apples. Bake 1 hour or until toothpick inserted into center comes out clean.

4. Immediately invert cake onto serving plate; let stand without removing pan about 5 minutes. Remove side and bottom of pan; let cool completely.

5. For sauce, combine butter and ½ cup brown sugar in small microwavable bowl; cover with plastic wrap. Microwave on HIGH 1 minute. Stir; microwave 30 seconds or until melted and well blended. Carefully, stir whiskey into butter mixture.

6. Starting at outer edges of cake, spoon whiskey sauce over entire cake, allowing sauce to run down side. *Makes 12 servings*

Spicy Apple Upside
Down Cake

Creamy Rice Pudding

1½ cups water
 ½ cup long grain rice*
 1 cinnamon stick
 1 (1-inch) piece orange or lemon peel
   Dash salt
 1 (14-ounce) can EAGLE BRAND® Sweetened Condensed Milk
   (NOT evaporated milk)
 ½ cup raisins or pecan halves (optional)
   Ground cinnamon

DO NOT use quick cooking rice.

1. In medium saucepan, combine water, rice, cinnamon stick, orange peel and salt. Bring to a boil; reduce heat. Cover and simmer 15 minutes.

2. Stir in EAGLE BRAND®. Cook uncovered over low heat, stirring frequently 25 minutes or until rice is tender. Remove cinnamon stick and orange peel. Cool. (Pudding will thicken as it cools.) Stir in raisins or nuts (optional). Serve warm or chilled. Garnish with cinnamon. Store leftovers covered in refrigerator. *Makes 4 (½-cup) servings*

Prep Time: 5 minutes
Cook Time: 40 minutes

Easy Holiday Shortbread Dough

 1 cup (2 sticks) unsalted butter, softened
 ½ cup powdered sugar
 2 tablespoons packed light brown sugar
 ¼ teaspoon salt
 2 cups all-purpose flour

1. Beat butter, sugars and salt in large bowl with electric mixer at medium speed until light and fluffy. Add flour, ½ cup at a time, beating well after each addition.

2. Form dough into ball; shape into 14-inch log. Wrap log tightly in plastic wrap. Refrigerate 1 hour.

3. Preheat oven to 300°F. Cut log into ½-inch-thick slices; place on ungreased cookie sheets. Bake 20 to 25 minutes or until lightly browned. Cool 5 minutes on cookie sheets. Remove to wire racks to cool completely. *Makes 28 cookies*

Cranberry Bread Pudding

1 quart milk

2 cups sugar

1 cup dried sweetened cranberries

5 eggs, lightly beaten

2 tablespoons vanilla

1 tablespoon baking powder

½ teaspoon ground cinnamon

1 loaf (16 ounces) French bread, torn in small pieces

Brandy Sauce

1½ cups sugar

1 cup butter or margarine

½ cup milk

½ to ¾ cup brandy

1. Preheat oven to 350°F. Spray 13×9-inch baking dish with nonstick cooking spray.

2. Combine 1 quart milk, 2 cups sugar, cranberries, eggs, vanilla, baking powder and cinnamon in large bowl; stir until well blended. Add bread and toss to blend thoroughly. Pour mixture into prepared dish. Bake 50 to 70 minutes or until golden and knife inserted into center comes out clean.

3. To make Brandy Sauce, combine 1½ cups sugar, butter and ½ cup milk in small saucepan. Heat over medium-high heat, stirring frequently, until butter melts and sugar dissolves. Remove from heat. Carefully, stir in brandy.

4. Cut bread pudding into squares. Spoon sauce over each serving.

Makes 12 servings

Luck o' the Irish Cupcakes

1 package (18¼ ounces) cake mix (any flavor), plus ingredients to
    prepare mix
1 container (16 ounces) white frosting
1 tube (4¼ ounces) green decorating icing with tip
   Green and orange sprinkles, decors and sugars

1. Preheat oven to 350°F. Line 24 standard (2½-inch) muffin pan cups
with decorative paper baking cups. Prepare cake mix according to
package directions. Spoon batter into prepared muffin cups, filling
two-thirds full.

2. Bake 15 to 20 minutes or until toothpick inserted into centers
comes out clean. Cool in pans on wire racks 10 minutes. Remove
cupcakes to racks; cool completely.

3. Frost cupcakes. Use icing to pipe Irish words (Slainte, Blarney, etc.)
or shamrock designs onto cupcakes as desired. Decorate with
sprinkles, decors and sugars as desired. *Makes 24 cupcakes*

Honey Shortbread

1 cup butter
⅓ cup honey
1 teaspoon vanilla
2½ cups all-purpose flour
¾ cup chopped pecans

Preheat oven to 300°F. Beat butter, honey and vanilla in large bowl
with electric mixer at medium speed until mixture is light and fluffy.
Add flour, 1 cup at a time, beating well after each addition. If dough
becomes too stiff to stir, knead in remaining flour by hand. Knead in
nuts. Pat dough into shortbread mold or ungreased 9-inch cast iron
skillet. Score surface with knife so it can be divided into 24 wedges.
With fork, prick deeply into the scores.

Bake 35 to 40 minutes. Cool in pan on wire rack 10 minutes. Remove
from pan. Cut into wedges while warm. *Makes 2 dozen wedges*

Favorite recipe from **National Honey Board**

Special Dark® Chocolate Chip Scones

3¼ cups all-purpose flour
½ cup sugar
1 tablespoon plus 1 teaspoon baking powder
¼ teaspoon salt
2 cups (12-ounce package) HERSHEY'S SPECIAL DARK®
   Chocolate Chips
½ cup chopped nuts (optional)
2 cups whipping cream, chilled
2 tablespoons butter, melted
   Additional sugar
   Powdered sugar (optional)

1. Heat oven to 375°F. Lightly grease 2 baking sheets.

2. Stir together flour, ½ cup sugar, baking powder and salt in large bowl. Stir in chocolate chips and nuts, if desired.

3. Stir whipping cream into flour mixture just until ingredients are moistened.

4. Turn mixture out onto lightly floured surface. Knead gently until soft dough forms, about 2 minutes. Divide dough into three equal balls. One ball at a time, flatten into 7-inch circle; cut into 8 triangles. Transfer triangles to prepared baking sheets, spacing 2 inches apart. Brush with melted butter and sprinkle with additional sugar.

5. Bake 15 to 20 minutes or until lightly browned. Serve warm, sprinkled with powdered sugar, if desired.   *Makes 24 scones*

Acknowledgments

The publisher would like to thank the companies listed below for the use of their recipes and photos in this publication.

Australian Lamb

Birds Eye Foods

EAGLE BRAND®

The Hershey Company

The Hidden Valley® Food Products Company

Hillshire Farm®

Hormel Foods, LLC

Mott's® is a registered trademark of Mott's, LLP

Mrs. Dash®

National Honey Board

Plochman, Inc.

Unilever

USA Rice Federation

Index